# CARD TRICKERY

## THROW, FAN, FLOURISH, SPOT CHEATERS, AND DO MAGIC WITH CARDS

**KLUTZ**®

# CONTENTS

① BEGINNER
② INTERMEDIATE
③ ADVANCED

# A BEGINNER'S GUIDE TO CARD RAZZLE-DAZZLE

**E**verything you need to rule any deck of cards is here, including the deck of cards. The cards are bridge-sized — narrower than a standard deck — which makes learning some tricks easier. Also included are two extra-special tricky cards too secret to talk about here. (See page 46.)

# BE ASTOUNDING

# BUT READ THIS FIRST

## OUR RATING SYSTEM

**DIFFICULTY 1 FACTOR** You'll be doing this like a pro in under five minutes.

**DIFFICULTY 2 FACTOR** Five minutes gets you started, but you'll need several follow-up sessions.

**DIFFICULTY 3 FACTOR** Getting this showstopper right will take a lot of work and practice — time well spent.

To minimize possible frustration, we recommend short and frequent practice sessions.

# ABOUT YOUR CARDS

These cards are bridge-sized cards, which are a little narrower than poker-sized cards.

Right out of the box, cards are stiff and flat, perfect for throwing. (A bent corner or card can ruin an otherwise fabulous throw.)

Old, well-worn cards aren't as good for throwing — but they bend well,

Your hand doesn't look exactly like the one in the picture. Everyone's hands are different. As you try these tricks, adjust our instructions to suit your hands.

which makes learning some other tricks easier. Find an old deck for shuffling practice. If you want to use a new deck for shuffling or springing (see page 22), break the cards in by flexing them one way and then the other to work out the stiffness.

# •• VOCABULARY ••

## Squaring the deck

means pushing all the cards together to make a neat rectangle, with no cards sticking out.

## Cutting the cards

means splitting the deck into two parts and then restacking it to change the cards that are on top.

# THROWING CARDS

**B**ack in the 1880s, magician Alexander Herrmann figured out how to throw playing cards from the stage to the back of the theater.

Some claim that the history of throwing cards began long before Herrmann, with the ninja of ancient Japan. These skilled assassins threw the *shuriken*, a flat metal weapon.

Card-throwing expert Ricky Jay, author of **Cards as Weapons**, can throw a card that travels 190 feet (58 m), moving up to 90 miles (144 km) per hour. From ten paces away, he can pierce the rind of a watermelon.

Reading this book won't make you a trained card assassin. But with a little practice, any klutz can send a card spinning through the air.

Magician Harry Thurston sold ad space on the cards he tossed into the audience at his shows.

Don't ever throw cards at people!

*With very little effort,
you can send a
card soaring.*

# The Ever-So-Easy
# Tap & Spin

**1** Pinch a card very lightly
between your left
thumb and
index finger,
like this:

About
2 inches
(5 cm)

**2** Hold your right index finger
**below** the card as shown.

**3** Move your finger **up** and gently
tap the card. Let go at
the same time.

**4** The card will fly
upward, spinning
beautifully.

**OR
NOT**

If not, try again.
You have a deck of
cards and you're
not afraid to
use them.

Spin gives the card
stability in flight.

If your card flies sideways, rather than
upward, concentrate on letting go the
moment your finger taps the card.

## YOUR FIRST CHALLENGE
# Catching It

*What goes up must come down.*
*Now you have a new challenge: catching it.*

If you do this effortlessly, go to the next page.
If not, we have a few tips.

### Swoop your hand over to the card and snatch it out of the air.

Bring your thumb and fingers together to pinch the card as you catch it.

Don't simply get your hand under the card and expect it to land there neatly. It won't. It will bounce away. You'll frantically grab for it with your other hand. It will bounce away again.

This way lies madness. You will flail madly. The card will end up on the floor. To avoid this, see the next tip.

### Remain calm.

Relax. Take deep breaths. It's only a card. You have plenty more. You can drop a few. You will drop more than a few.

### Keep your eye on the card.

It's easy to forget this in the heat of the moment.

*You're going to send a card spinning through the air and have it come right back to you. Thanks to all your catching practice, you'll then pluck that card neatly from the air, smiling all the while.*

## The Basic Throw

**1** Pinch a card lightly as shown.

Your thumb has to be exactly here.

**2** Cock your wrist and gently flick it to send the card up. At the same time, **pull down** on the corner with your index finger to give the card a spin.

The other side

Pull with your finger.

Use your wrist, not your arm.

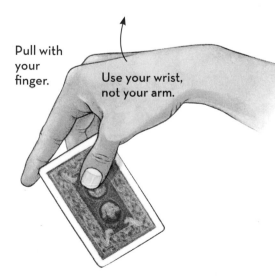

Focus on making the card spin. Don't shoot for the stars. Toss it up to just above eye level. Do it again. And again. And again.

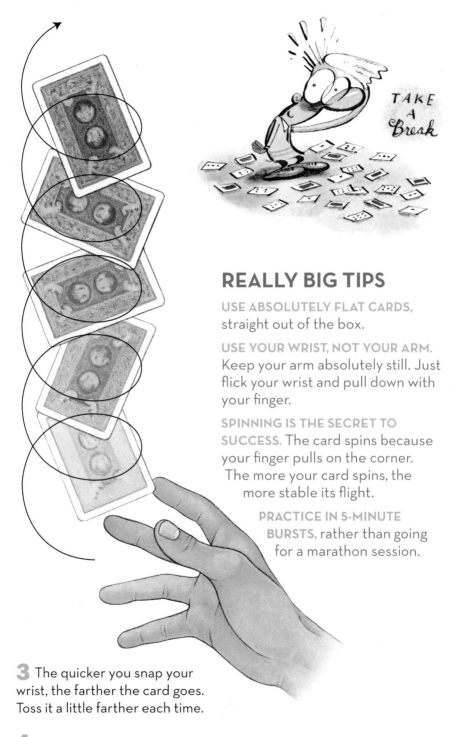

TAKE A Break

## REALLY BIG TIPS

**USE ABSOLUTELY FLAT CARDS,** straight out of the box.

**USE YOUR WRIST, NOT YOUR ARM.** Keep your arm absolutely still. Just flick your wrist and pull down with your finger.

**SPINNING IS THE SECRET TO SUCCESS.** The card spins because your finger pulls on the corner. The more your card spins, the more stable its flight.

**PRACTICE IN 5-MINUTE BURSTS,** rather than going for a marathon session.

**3** The quicker you snap your wrist, the farther the card goes. Toss it a little farther each time.

**4** Keep practicing until you can toss the card up and catch it when it comes down. When you've achieved this, move on to the next page.

DIFFICULTY **2** FACTOR

## spin

· GOING FURTHER ·
# BOOMERANG

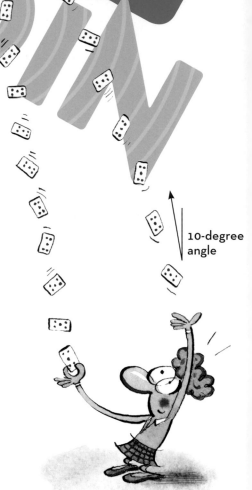

10-degree angle

*Practice the basic boomerang spin until you can toss a card up and catch it neatly.*

*That's cool, but to make the trick more impressive, you need to throw the card upward at an angle — and have it return to you.*

**1** Stand up. You want to be mobile for this trick.

**2** Rather than throwing the card straight up, throw it up **at an angle** that's just 10 degrees away from the vertical. The card will come back at a lower angle. You may have to take a step forward to catch it.

**3** Try again, this time increasing the angle to 20 or 30 degrees from the vertical.

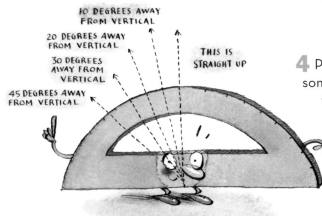

10 DEGREES AWAY FROM VERTICAL

20 DEGREES AWAY FROM VERTICAL

30 DEGREES AWAY FROM VERTICAL

45 DEGREES AWAY FROM VERTICAL

THIS IS STRAIGHT UP

**4** Practice, practice, and practice some more. Experiment to find the angle that works for you. Once you've found an angle that works, throw the card a little farther.

# ≈ ZEN ≈
## AND THE ART OF
# THROWING CARDS

*Here's the Klutz step-by-step path to card-throwing enlightenment.*

**1** To turn your boomerang spin into a long-distance throw, change the angle of your toss. Throw a card as far as you can.

For a boomerang spin, choose an angle in this range.

For a card that doesn't come back, you want an angle more like this.

**2** Did your card skim through the air? Or did it flutter to the ground in a most annoying fashion?

Most people throw hard when they want to throw far. But throwing cards is not about muscle. It's all about spin.

**3** To improve your long-distance throw, you need to make sure that every card you throw is spinning madly. To manage that, you need to focus on your technique. So take a deep breath, relax, and turn the page.

# ZEN
## AND THE ART OF
# THROWING CARDS
(continued)

**4** Hold the card in the grip you used for the boomerang spin (page 10). Turn your hand so the face of the card is parallel to the floor.

**5** Extend your arm. Bend it a little. Cock your wrist slightly.

**6** Pull back on the corner of your card with your finger and flick your wrist as you let go of the card. **Don't try for distance.** This is all about **spin.**

**7** Keep practicing until every card you throw is spinning madly.

**8** To add distance, flick your wrist harder when you pull with your finger. At the same time, pull your hand back toward your body as you let go. Pulling your hand back will feel odd. But it adds to the spin — and the card will fly away faster.

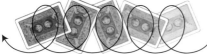

**HELPFUL TIPS**

• Short practice sessions are best.

• If your card flutters when you throw, return to step 4 and work on your spin.

*A card flies best when it's spinning like a helicopter rotor.*

# HAT-TOSS GAME

*This time-honored time waster is a great way to practice spinning cards.*

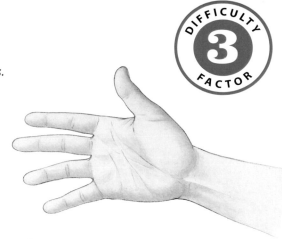

**YOU'LL NEED** a hat — ideally, one with a brim. If you can't find a hat, substitute a bowl, wastebasket, or bucket.

**1** Set the hat upside down on the floor. To make the game easier, put the hat in a corner. For a challenge, put it in the middle of the room.

**2** Give each player ten cards.

**3** Taking turns, each player tries to toss a card into the hat from a few paces away. Play until all players have thrown all their cards.

**4** Here's how to keep score.

| If a card... | you get... |
|---|---|
| misses the hat | 0 points |
| lands on the brim | 1 point |
| lands in the hat | 2 points |

**Any card** that lands in the hat during your turn earns you two points. Suppose your card knocks a card into the hat then lands on the brim. That's two points for the card in the hat and one point for the one that landed on the brim.

# SHUFFLES, FANS, AND FLOURISHES

**T**o handle cards with confidence, you need to know how to shuffle, cut the cards, fan the deck, and maybe do a few fancy flourishes as well. Flourishes are show-off moves that people use to demonstrate their skill with cards. .

Some folks specialize in the art of **Extreme Card Manipulation** (XCM). The amazing and flashy flourishes of XCM are designed to astound an audience with dexterity and style.

We'll teach you the moves you need to get started. To become a real card pro, you'll need to practice until you can make all these moves without thinking twice.

## MECHANIC'S GRIP

A mechanic is a card cheater specializing in sneaky dealing and sleight of hand. But even people who aren't sneaky dealers use this grip.

## BIDDLE GRIP

The biddle grip (named after magician Elmer Biddle) is used in many shuffles and cuts.

# ribbon SPREAD

*You can spread the cards on any table in a single, dramatic gesture.*

**1** Hold the cards in your right hand in a biddle grip. (See page 17.) Move your index finger so that it's on the long side of the deck.

**2** Set the cards on the table and sweep your right hand from left to right, using your index finger to release cards as the deck moves. Can you create a ribbon of evenly spaced cards on the table?

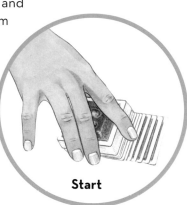

**Start**

**Finish**

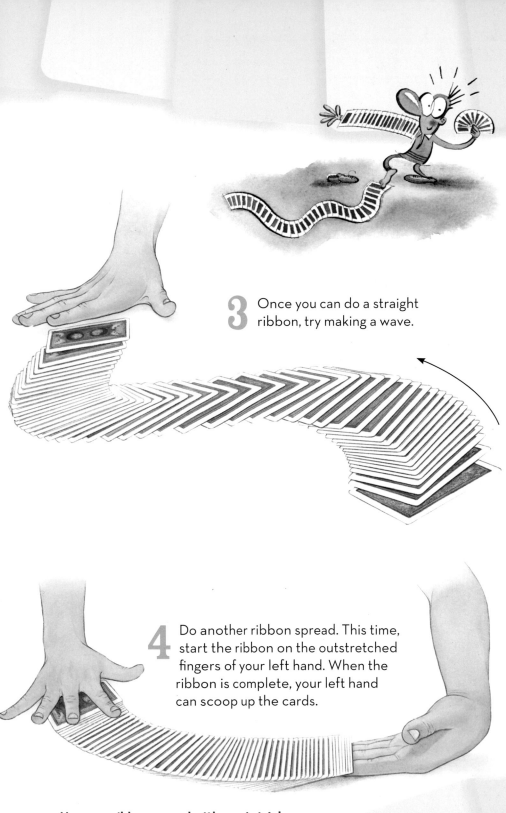

**3** Once you can do a straight ribbon, try making a wave.

**4** Do another ribbon spread. This time, start the ribbon on the outstretched fingers of your left hand. When the ribbon is complete, your left hand can scoop up the cards.

Use your ribbon spread with magic tricks.
See pages 50, 51, and 58.

# FANCY
## RIBBON WORK

*To get fancy with your ribbon work, you need a surface that's covered with felt, velvet, or some other material that keeps the cards from sliding. Try these moves on a velveteen bedspread or a carpet without much nap.*

**1** Ribbon spread the cards with the fingers of your left hand under the beginning of the ribbon. With your left hand, push up the card at the start of the ribbon so that it's vertical...

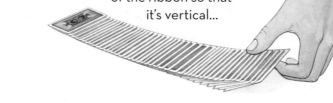

**2** ...then push it over.

**3** The whole ribbon will turn over in a graceful wave.

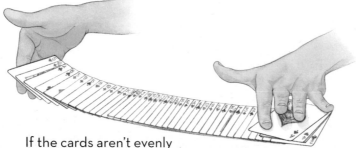

If the cards aren't evenly spaced, the wave may break halfway down the ribbon. If that happens, try again.

**4** Try steps 1, 2, and 3 again, but this time put your right hand right beside the end of the ribbon, so that the cards turn over into your right hand. Then you can scoop the cards up with your right hand.

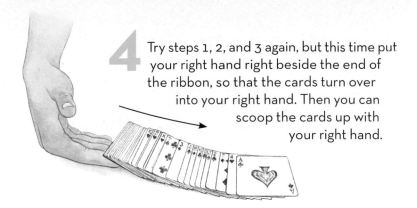

### TROUBLESHOOTING
If you forget to start the ribbon on your fingers, pick up the last card in the ribbon and slide it under the first card.

Use this card to flip the ribbon over.

**A BONUS CHALLENGE**
Here's something that's tough even for card experts.

Try doing a ribbon spread on your arm.

DIFFICULTY **3** FACTOR

*Send cards jumping dramatically from hand to hand. This is the hardest trick (but one of the coolest) in the book.*

# SPRINGING THE CARDS

It's easiest to learn this trick with a well-worn, broken-in deck of cards.

**1** Hold ten to twenty cards in your right hand and squeeze them so that the cards bend toward your hand.

**The edges of the cards are at the tips of your fingers and thumb.**

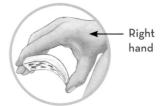

Right hand

**2** Your left hand will catch the cards. Spread your fingers, but keep them cupped. Put your pinky against your stomach.

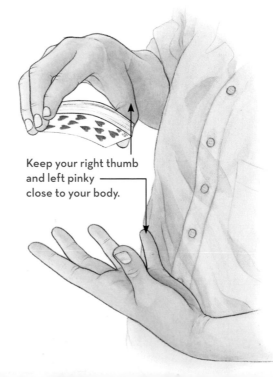

Keep your right thumb and left pinky close to your body.

**3** Place your right hand (which is holding the cards) just a few inches (about 10 cm) above your left hand.

**The first time you try this, the cards will fly all over the room. Count on it. (Sorry.)**

**4** Let the cards slip off the tip of your thumb and spring into your waiting hand.

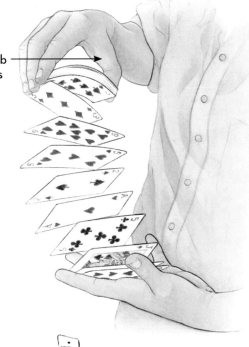

Thumb points down

**5** Try again. This time, point your right thumb toward the palm of your left hand. Keep both hands close to you so your body acts as a backboard.

**7** Work on controlling the flow so that cards spring one after the other without a pause.

**8** Practice, practice, practice.

---

## TROUBLESHOOTING

◆ Be sure the cards are slipping off your thumb. If the cards won't slip off your thumb, move the edges of the cards closer to the tip of your thumb.

◆ Practice for no more than ten minutes, then take a break. It'll take many practice sessions to get good at this.

**More tips on the next page.**

*more tips on*

# SPRINGING
## THE CARDS

*Learning to spring cards
can take weeks of practice.
Don't get discouraged.*

If you're tired of picking up cards off the floor, practice over a bed or a couch.

If you're springing 10 cards, try 20. If you're springing 20, try 30. Eventually use the whole deck.

When you're ready, try moving your hands away from your body.

Use your pinky to keep the cards from sliding off your left hand.

Some magicians let the cards slip off their fingers rather than their thumb. This will send the cards shooting away from you. Bend the fingers of your catching hand so the cards don't slide off.

### WHEN YOU'RE READY FOR A CHALLENGE

Move your hands farther apart. Pros start with their hands close together, spread their hands apart as the cards spring, and then bring their hands back together at the end. Give that a try.

# ONE-HAND FAN

If you can snap your fingers, you can spread the cards into a beautiful fan with one hand.

**1** Hold your right hand out with your fingers flat. Place half the deck against your hand, like this.

**2** Move your thumb in the direction of the arrow. Your thumb moves much as it would if you were snapping your fingers — but the cards are between your thumb and your fingers. So rather than snapping your fingers, your thumb fans the cards.

25

# One-Hand Cut

*Here's a fancy way to cut the cards. Magicians call this the Charlier cut.*

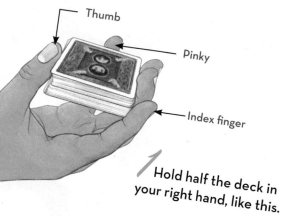

THWACK

**When you hold the deck in your right hand, you see this.**

Index finger

Pinky

Thumb

Thumb

Pinky

**Someone watching you sees this**

Index finger

*1* Hold half the deck in your right hand, like this.

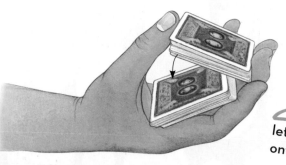

*2* Shift your thumb to let half the cards drop onto your palm.

Tilt the deck a little so your pinky is on the downhill side.

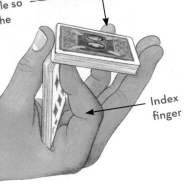

*3* Use your index finger to push up the bottom cards until the two halves are at right angles.

Index finger

Your pinky helps control the cards.

*4* Let the bottom half slip past the top half. The top half will slide down to rest on your index finger.

*5* Use your thumb to push the cards that were on the bottom onto the top. This completes the cut.

You have to learn this trick by feel. You won't be able to see what your index finger is doing — unless you look in a mirror.

When you're ready, try doing this cut with the whole deck.

# *honest* OVERHAND
## SHUFFLE

*This easy-to-learn shuffle*
*mixes cards without bending them.*

**1** Hold the deck in your right hand, as shown. Using your left thumb, slide the first few cards from the top of the deck into your left hand.

The cards slide off the top of the deck into your left hand.

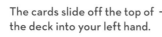

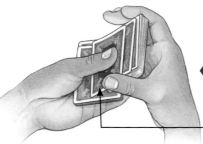

**2** Lift your right hand clear of your left, then repeat the move from step 1.

The next few cards land on top of the others.

**3** Keep sliding packets of cards from the stack in your right hand to the stack in your left hand...

...until the whole deck is in your left hand.

**Card expert John Scarne calls this shuffle "the stumble bum cheat's best friend." See page 37 to learn why.**

# RIFFLING THE CARDS

*For a great shuffle, you must learn to riffle the cards. Riffling means letting the cards flip through your fingers one by one.*

**1** Hold the deck in your left hand and set one end on the table. Tip the deck to the right so that the top slants to the right. Place your right thumb at the top of the deck.

The deck slants under your thumb.

Curl your right index finger. Rest your knuckle on the back of the deck.

**2** Pull back with your right thumb and push with your knuckle so that the cards bend. Move your thumb to release the cards. Practice until the cards escape your thumb one by one, purring like a cat.

### TROUBLESHOOTING

If the cards fall in clumps (rather than one by one), make sure the deck slants under your thumb. This makes it easier to release cards one at a time.

# DOVETAIL SHUFFLE

*Shuffle like a pro, using the method most card players prefer.*

Index fingers on top

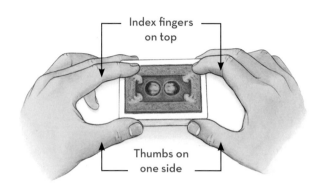

Thumbs on one side

**1** Start like this, with the deck on a table.

**2** Use your right thumb to split the deck in half.

**3** Grasp half the deck in each hand.

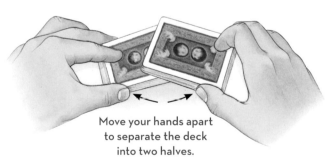

Move your hands apart to separate the deck into two halves.

## WHAT'S GOOD ABOUT IT?

THIS IS THE WAY THE PROS SHUFFLE.

## WHAT'S BAD ABOUT IT?

IT DOESN'T LOOK FLASHY.

**4** Use your thumbs to lift the corners of the cards while you push down with your index fingers.
The cards will bend.

Fingers push down

Thumbs lift corners

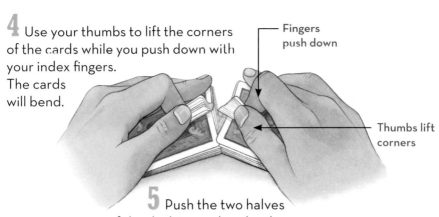

**5** Push the two halves of the deck toward each other. Riffle both halves of the deck at the same time, so that the corners of the cards overlap.

**6** You will end up with two packets of cards interlaced at the corners. Push the halves together and you have a shuffled deck.

# BEAUTIFUL !

If you have trouble, go back to page 29 and practice riffling.

**Don't help cheaters out by showing them cards when you shuffle. Use the dovetail shuffle to keep your bottom cards hidden from view.**

**For a dishonest version of the dovetail shuffle, see page 36.**

# RIFFLE SHUFFLE
## *with*
# WATERFALL
## *finish*

*This shuffle is easiest with old, flexible cards.*

### WHAT'S GOOD ABOUT IT?

IT LOOKS AND SOUNDS GREAT!

**1** Split the deck in half. Hold each half as shown.

> **This is what it looks like to someone watching you.**

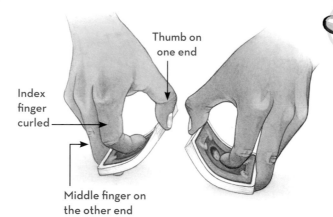

Thumb on one end

Index finger curled

Middle finger on the other end

### WHAT'S BAD ABOUT IT?

IT BENDS THE CARDS, WHICH IS NOT GOOD IF YOU WANT TO USE THE SAME CARDS FOR THROWING.

**2** Push down with your index fingers and pull back with your thumbs to bend the cards. Riffle the cards together.

The edges of the cards are at the tips of your thumbs.

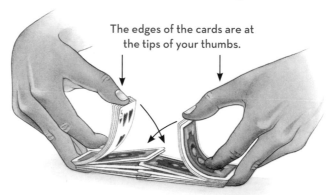

**3** Move all your fingers to the ends of the cards. Put both thumbs where the cards overlap.

Thumbs push down

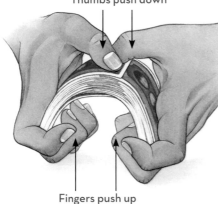

**4** Curl your fingers up and bend the outer edges of the cards down.

Fingers push up

**5** Uncurl your fingers and relax your grip on the cards. Let the cards spring together dramatically.

Push the cards together.

NICE JOB!

**TROUBLESHOOTING**
If you have trouble riffling the cards, go back to page 29 and practice riffling, or adjust the position of your thumbs and the angle of the cards. If you're using a new deck, bend the cards one way and then the other to break them in.

# how to spot
# CARD CHEATERS

**H**ere's a crash course on how people cheat at cards. Study up so you won't be bamboozled by their underhanded ways.

We give you complete instructions on how to do sneaky shuffles that you can use with magic tricks. Magicians aren't cheaters, even when they use marked cards or sneaky shuffles. When a magician does a magic trick, everyone knows that it's a trick. As a magician, you can fool people and still leave them happy. Isn't that a wonderful thing?

Five of these six cards are marked — the four aces and the queen of hearts. Can you spot the differences that reveal which card is which? See page 45 for the key.

SNEAKY
SHUFFLE
No. 1

## NOT-SO-HONEST
# DOVETAIL SHUFFLE

*A cheater (or a magician) can shuffle the deck
but leave some cards in the same place.*

**1** Get ready to do a
normal dovetail
shuffle (page 30)
or riffle shuffle
(page 32). When
you split the deck
in half, remember
which half was on top.

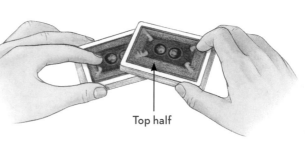

Top half

**2** When you shuffle, start with
the bottom half of the deck
and riffle it faster than the top.
You'll finish riffling the bottom
half first. This keeps up to
eight cards in the same
place at the top of the
deck. This is called
**controlling the top stock**.

**3** By riffling the
bottom half
first, you also keep
the bottom cards
unchanged. This is
called **controlling
the bottom stock.**

The top cards
are still on top.

## NOT-SO-HONEST
# OVERHAND SHUFFLE

*A cheater (or a magician) can move a card from
the bottom of the deck to the top, or vice versa.*

**1** In an honest overhand
shuffle (page 28), your
left thumb slides, or
*shuffles off,* packets
of cards from your right
hand to your left.

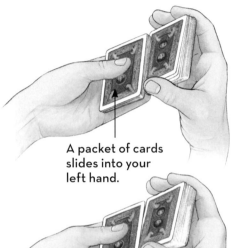

**A packet of cards
slides into your
left hand.**

**2** Try shuffling off one
card at a time. To
do this, press very lightly
on the cards with your
left thumb.

**One card slides
into your left hand.**

**3** When you can shuffle
off single cards easily,
square the deck and
sneakily peek at the
bottom card.

**4** Do a normal overhand
shuffle until the end. Shuffle
off the last few cards one at a
time. When you're done, the
bottom card will be on the top.

**5** To move that
card back to the
bottom, shuffle the cards
again, shuffling off the first
few cards one by one.

# BEATING THE CUT

*In many card games, the dealer shuffles and another player cuts the cards. A cheater who has put certain cards on the top or on the bottom must make sure that the cut doesn't mess up his plans.*

**PUT A CRIMP IN IT** A cheater can sneakily bend or crimp a card or a group of cards to make a break in the deck where he wants it cut. If he has a fellow cheater in the game, the crimp lets his pal cut in the perfect spot. Even an honest player is likely to cut at the crimped card.

**A SALTY MOVE** A cheater can make a break in the deck by dropping a few grains of salt from a pretzel onto the card she wants on top. She does one last cut, then gives someone else the cards to cut. The salt holds the cards apart a little bit, increasing the odds that the deck will be cut right where she wants.

**FAKING A CUT** Magicians sometimes pretend to cut the cards without actually doing it. To do a false cut, hold the deck in your left hand. With your right hand, slide the bottom half of the deck toward you. Looking at the audience, lift the bottom half of the deck over the deck and set it on the table in front of you. Take the top half of the deck with your right hand, and set it on top of the cards on the table. Most observers will think you cut the cards, but you didn't.

*Knowing your opponents' cards can give you the edge in any card game.*

*There are many ways for a cheating dealer to peek at a card in the deck.*

# SNEAKY PEEKING

When squaring the deck, a cheater can take a look at the bottom card.

In the back peek, the dealer uses his thumb to separate the top card from the rest.

When cutting the cards, a cheater can bend the cards just enough to reveal the bottom card.

You can use these sneaky peeks in magic tricks. See pages 54 and 56.

In a stacked deck, the cards are pre-arranged to give one or more players a big advantage. A cheater can sneakily stack a deck when gathering up cards at the end of a hand, putting certain cards on the top or bottom of the deck. This is called culling or rabbit hunting.

If you do successfully cut the cards, a sly cheater can do a sneaky bit of sleight of hand that lets him put the deck back the way it was. Cheaters call this a hop or elevator.

# A field guide to Card Sharks

🦈 SHARK NO. 1 🦈

## DOUBLE DEALER

Some cheaters specialize in **double dealing**, giving themselves extra cards.

### How does this work?

When dealing to himself, a double dealer secretly pushes off two cards. This gives him more chances to make a better hand. He disposes of the extra cards by sneakily stashing them up a sleeve, in a sock, or in some other hiding place.

Among cheaters, removing cards from the table is called **going south.** Cards that are hidden in a sock or a sleeve are called **hold outs**. Stealing cards from the table, hiding them, and using them later is called **hand mucking**. It's a common way to cheat.

### Spotting the Cheater

The best way to catch a double dealer who is hiding cards is to count the cards from time to time. If your deck is short a few cards, it's possible that a hold out artist is at work.

# NUMBER-TWO

A **number-two** man (or woman) specializes in **dealing seconds;** that is, dealing the second card in the deck while appearing to deal normally.

## How does this work?

Normally, a dealer holds the deck in his left hand and uses his left thumb to push out the top card so his right hand can take it. The number-two man pushes out the top card, then pulls it back with his left thumb while dealing the second card.

This lets him take the top card if he wants it. If he's playing with marked cards, he knows what card is on top. If the cards aren't marked, he may have slyly peeked at the card on top. Or maybe he knows what the top card is because he put it there with sneaky shuffling.

## Spotting the Cheater

Watch for a dealer with a **dead thumb** who tilts the deck so you can't see the top card. Usually, a dealer lifts his thumb slightly after he pushes out the top card. But most people who deal seconds keep their thumb in contact with the cards.

# CELLAR DEALER

A **cellar dealer** specializes in dealing from the bottom of the deck.

## HOW DOES THIS WORK?

Before dealing, the cellar dealer slyly arranges the deck so certain cards are on the bottom. Maybe the cheater spots an ace on the bottom of the deck and then adds a discarded hand with another ace. Maybe he has an ace up his sleeve from an earlier hand and puts that on the bottom, too. The cellar dealer can keep those aces together with a less-than-honest shuffle (page 36) and use some clever tricks to beat the cut (page 38).

When dealing, the cellar dealer can deal cards from the top of the deck to opponents and from the bottom to himself or a friend.

## SPOTTING THE CHEATER

Listen to the sound of the cards. Bottom dealing sounds different from honest dealing. Keep an eye on the cards. Sometimes, when a cellar dealer deals the bottom card, the card just above it is carried along and ends up sticking out from the rest of the deck. This is called a **hanger** and it's a sign of a cellar dealer at work. It's easiest to spot someone who is dealing from the bottom when you use a deck with one big picture on the back. You can see that the picture doesn't move as the cheater deals.

## SHARK NO. 4
# THE COOLER

In a stacked deck, the cards have been arranged in advance in a specific order. Some cheaters sneak a stacked deck into a game. The cheater's stacked deck is known as a **cold deck, cooler,** or **ice.**

### HOW DOES THIS WORK?

The cheater has to switch decks, substituting the stacked deck for the deck that's been in the game. Often, an accomplice helps by creating a distraction, spilling a drink to call everyone's attention away from the person who is switching the decks.

### SPOTTING THE CHEATER

Keep an eye out for distractions that might be providing cover for a deck switch. If someone spills a drink or brings in snacks, ask that the deck be shuffled and cut a few times before you start to play again.

## SHARK NO. 5
# TEAM SCHEME

Card sharks often swim in schools, working together to cheat honest players.

### HOW DOES THIS WORK?

With word codes, hand signals, and other secret signs, two or more cheaters can tell each other what cards they're holding. Using a word code, a cheater might say, "Beautiful, just beautiful."

This lets her pals know that she has a queen and a jack of the same suit. Often, partners in the team scheme have agreed that only the cheater with the best cards will play the hand.

## SHARK NO. 6
# PAPER WORKER

From the back, all the cards in the deck are supposed to look the same. A **paper worker** marks the backs of the cards so she can tell them apart.

## HOW DOES THIS WORK?

There are dozens of different ways to mark cards so most people won't notice. Cheaters can:

- ink a small mark on the card's border (**border work**)
- remove parts of the printed design (**cutout work**)
- darken or bleach portions of the cards (**shading**)
- scratch, nick, dent, or bend the cards while playing with them
- smudge the cards with **daub**, goop that leaves a mark on the cards
- make marks that can only be read through special glasses or contact lenses (known as **luminous readers**)

A cheater may also use **trims** or **strippers**, cards that are shorter or narrower than regular cards, or tapered. The physical differences between these cards and the rest of the deck make it easier to cut to these cards or separate them from the rest of the deck.

## SPOTTING THE CHEATER

One way to check cards for visible markings is to "take them to the movies." Riffle through the deck as if the cards were pages in a flip book. If all the cards are identical, it'll be like watching a still picture. But if there are marks, you'll see them jumping around as you flip through the deck.

# GLIM WORKER

A **glim worker** uses a **shiner**, a reflective object that acts like a mirror, letting the cheater see cards as she deals them.

## HOW DOES THIS WORK?

The glim worker brings a shiner to the game. The ideal shiner is something that you wouldn't think twice about seeing on a card table: a polished metal pocket watch, a pair of sunglasses, anything that can act like a mirror.

When the glim worker is dealing the cards, the shiner reflects the hidden side of the cards. The cheater watches the reflections and knows who is getting which cards.

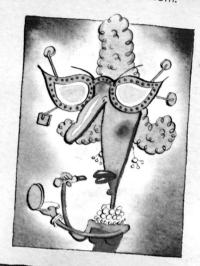

## SPOTTING THE CHEATER

The best way to catch a dealer who is using a shiner is to watch her eyes. The dealer will be looking at the shiner, not at the cards.

Even if the glim worker doesn't know everyone's cards, just knowing a few of the cards in people's hands can help the cheater win.

## MARKED CARDS

Five of these six cards are marked — the four aces and the queen of hearts.

Take a look at the sunburst in the corner of each card. On clubs, diamonds, and hearts, a cheater used blue to fill in some of the white rays. The position of the rays that have been colored reveals the suit. (On spades, no rays are filled in.)

To tell a card's rank, look at the top border. One bar is filled in with blue to indicate the aces; a different one is filled in to indicate the queen.

Ace of clubs

Ace of diamonds

Ace of hearts

Ace of spades

Queen of hearts

Unmarked card

# GLIM WORKER

A **glim worker** uses a **shiner,** a reflective object that acts like a mirror, letting the cheater see cards as she deals them.

## HOW DOES THIS WORK?

The glim worker brings a shiner to the game. The ideal shiner is something that you wouldn't think twice about seeing on a card table: a polished metal pocket watch, a pair of sunglasses, anything that can act like a mirror.

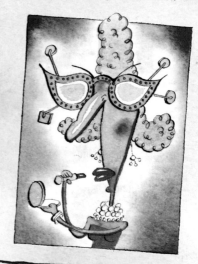

When the glim worker is dealing the cards, the shiner reflects the hidden side of the cards. The cheater watches the reflections and knows who is getting which cards.

## SPOTTING THE CHEATER

The best way to catch a dealer who is using a shiner is to watch her eyes. The dealer will be looking at the shiner, not at the cards.

Even if the glim worker doesn't know everyone's cards, just knowing a few of the cards in people's hands can help the cheater win.

## MARKED CARDS

Five of these six cards are marked — the four aces and the queen of hearts.

Take a look at the sunburst in the corner of each card. On clubs, diamonds, and hearts, a cheater used blue to fill in some of the white rays. The position of the rays that have been colored reveals the suit. (On spades, no rays are filled in.)

To tell a card's rank, look at the top border. One bar is filled in with blue to indicate the aces; a different one is filled in to indicate the queen.

Ace of clubs

Ace of diamonds

Ace of hearts

Ace of spades

Queen of hearts

Unmarked card

# Magic

**★ WITH CARDS ★**

**S**top! Before reading further, you must understand what it means to become a magician.

You must lie. With a straight face, you must talk about psychic vibrations, mind reading, and other malarkey.

While telling unbelievable fibs, you must keep your mind on what you're really doing: distracting the audience from your sneaky moves — without distracting yourself.

You must practice every trick before showing it to an audience. Practice your lies (more politely known as **patter**) as well as your sneaky moves.

Finally, you must abide by the Magician's Oath. Break this oath and your amazing magic will become a handful of cheap tricks — and no one likes a cheap trick.

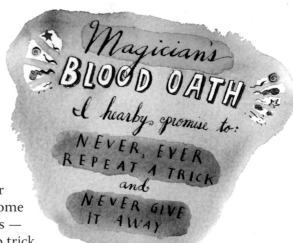

Magician's BLOOD OATH

I hearby promise to:

NEVER, EVER REPEAT A TRICK

and

NEVER GIVE IT AWAY

# HIDE &SEEK

*One sneaky move is all it takes to baffle people with this mystifying trick.*

## WHAT THE AUDIENCE SEES

You show the audience two cards: the queen of hearts and the jack of spades. Saying that these cards like to play hide-and-seek, you hide the queen behind your back. When you ask the audience which card is hiding, they are sure it's the queen.

But the cards have switched places; the jack is behind your back. Hide the jack and it magically becomes the queen.

## WHAT YOU NEED

A double-faced card and a double-backed card. You'll find both in the envelope on page 46.

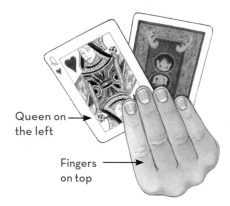

Queen on the left

Fingers on top

## PRACTICE THIS SNEAKY MOVE

**1** Hold the cards in your **right** hand like this. Be sure your palm faces downward and the cards are parallel to the floor.

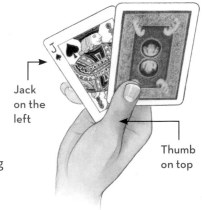

Jack on the left

Thumb on top

**2** Flip your hand over so your palm faces up. At the same time, slide your thumb to the right so the cards switch position.

**3** Flip your hand over again, sliding your thumb to the left. The cards return to their original position.

**4** Practice until you can do this move while talking nonstop.

**1** Hold the cards in your right hand with the queen on top and the cards parallel to the floor.

**2** While talking about how these cards play hide-and-seek, use your sneaky move to show the audience the jack.

**3** Still talking, use your sneaky move to return the cards to their original position, with the queen showing.

**4** Say, "It's the queen's turn to hide." Take the queen in your left hand. Keep the queen facing the audience as you put the card behind your back. Behind your back, turn the card over so the jack will show. Keep holding the double-backed card in front of you.

**5** Ask the audience, "Who is hiding?" When they say, "The queen," bring out the jack.

**6** Put the jack at a 45-degree angle on top of and to the left of the card in your hand, just as the queen was at the beginning.

**7** Repeat the same procedure, putting the jack behind your back — then bringing out the queen.

Some magicians call this trick "Two-Card Monte." Three-Card Monte is traditionally played by con artists on street corners. The con artist shows you the queen, then moves three cards around really fast and challenges you to find the queen. You can't. There's only one way to win at Three-Card Monte: **Don't play.**

# MYSTERY FLiP

*Place a packet of cards face to face with the remainder of the deck.
Magically, the cards flip over so that they all face the same way.*

**1** Sneakily put the double-backed card on the bottom of the deck.

**2** Hold the deck in your left hand. Have a volunteer cut off a packet of cards.

Your left hand

**3** Take the packet of cards from the volunteer with your right hand. At the same time, sneakily turn your left hand over so your palm faces down.

Double-backed card

Your left hand

**4** Place the volunteer's cards face up, under the cards in your hand.

**5** Square the deck. Turn it over in your hands three times. The double-backed card is on the bottom again.

**6** Do a ribbon spread (page 18) to show that the cards all face the same way.

This is the double-backed card.

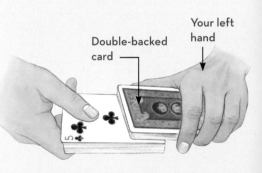

**7** Sneak the double-backed card off the bottom of the deck.

# WHICH WAY IS UP?

*Volunteers choose cards. You lose those cards in the deck, and then spread the cards on the table. Voilà! Only the chosen cards are face up.*

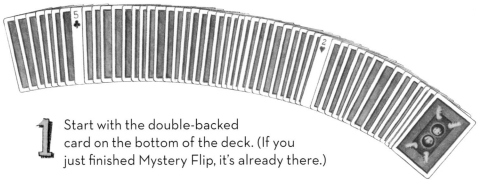

**1** Start with the double-backed card on the bottom of the deck. (If you just finished Mystery Flip, it's already there.)

**2** Fan the deck and have a few volunteers choose cards.

**3** Square the deck in your left hand with your palm facing up. While the volunteers show their cards to the audience, drop your left hand to your side.

**4** Bring your hand back up with your palm facing down. The double-backed card makes the deck look right side up.

**5** One by one, take the cards from your volunteers. Slide each card into the middle of the deck. Don't let the audience see that the cards below the top card are face up.

Double-backed card

SHAZAM!
SHISHKABOB!
ALLEYOOPS!

**6** Now you need to flip the deck over again. Ask everyone to chant a magic word while you and your volunteers spin around three times. When your back is to the audience, turn the deck over.

**7** Spread the deck. Every card is face down except for the chosen cards. For a flashy finale, use a ribbon spread (page 18).

**8** Sneakily remove the double-backed card before moving on to another trick.

## OOPS! I LOST MY TRICK CARD

*You can do this trick without a trick card.*

While your volunteers are showing their cards to the audience, secretly flip the bottom card over. Then turn the deck over so the back of the bottom card is facing up.

"I'M turning MY BACK so I CAN'T SEE your CARDS"

Follow the other steps with just one change: In step 6, turn the deck over and flip the bottom card the right way around while spinning and chanting the magic word. Make your move when your back is to the audience.

**OOPS! I LOST MY TRICK CARD (Option 2)** You can make a double-backed card for any deck. Just glue the deck's jokers face to face.

# Is This Your Card?

Someone chooses a card but doesn't show it to the magician. The magician does some magical stuff and reveals the chosen card.

Hundreds of card tricks follow this script. What makes one trick stand out? The magician's method of revealing the card. A magician who shuffles through the deck and then asks, "Is this your card?" sends the audience away yawning.

Once you understand the key card principle, you can use it to invent your own card tricks.

In the next three tricks, you find a chosen card using the key card principle. In each trick, you reveal the card in a different amusing or startling way. That's what makes each trick special.

# CIRCUS SWINDLE

DIFFICULTY FACTOR **1**

*In the late 1800s, cheaters prowled the circus midway, duping the unwary with this trick. It's still a fine way to startle (but not swindle) your friends.*

**1** Shuffle the cards. When you square the cards, take a peek at the bottom one. This is your **key card.**

**2** Have a volunteer pick a card, show it to everyone (except you, of course), put it on top of the deck, and then cut the cards.

**3** Ask the audience to concentrate on the chosen card while you turn the cards over, one by one. You are looking for the key card.

**This is what someone watching you sees.**

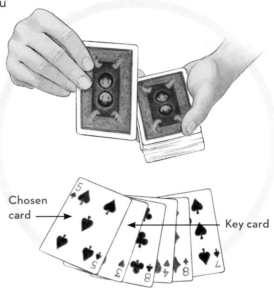

**4** When you turn over the key card, the next card will be the chosen card. **Don't stop.** Keep turning over cards. Your audience will be sure you've botched the trick.

Chosen card →

← Key card

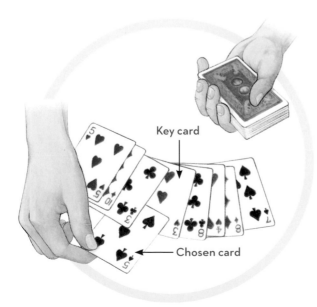

Key card

Chosen card

**5** A few cards past the chosen card, say, "The next card I turn over will be the card you chose."

**6** Grab the chosen card and turn it over. It's face up and you're turning it face down — but you're definitely turning it over.

# LEVITATING CARD

*Make a chosen card rise mysteriously from the deck.*

**1** Shuffle the cards. Peek at the bottom card when you square them. This is your **key card.**

**2** Have a volunteer pick a card and rub it on his hair to give it a static charge.

Chosen card

Key card

**3** Have the volunteer put his card on top of the deck and cut the cards a few times.

**4** With the faces toward you, fan through the cards. Tell the audience that you are feeling for the static charge. Actually, you're looking for the key card.

The chosen card will be to the right of the key card as you fan from bottom to top.

**5** You want to cut between the key card and the chosen card. Fan a few cards, take them into your right hand, and move them to the top of the deck. Do this a few times. Make sure your last cut puts the chosen card on top.

**6** Tell the audience that you'll use the static charge on the card to make it rise from the deck. Rub your right index finger on your hair, saying you need to charge it.

**7** Face the audience, holding the deck in your left hand with the backs toward you. Tilt the top of the cards toward you.

**8** Tap on the top of the deck with your finger, as if you're trying to make the card move. At first, it doesn't work. Rub your finger on your hair again.

**What the audience sees**

**9** Secretly, hidden behind the deck, extend your pinky. Push against the back of the chosen card with your pinky as you move your hand upward. Your pinky will move the card upward. To the audience, it will look like the card is rising, attracted by your pointing finger.

**What you do**

# *Feel the* BEAT

*Find the chosen card by sensing which card has matching psychic vibrations — or so you say.*

*1* Shuffle the deck. Use a fancy shuffle, if you like.

*2* Ribbon spread the deck face up (see page 18). The card that's on the bottom of the deck is your **key card.**

*3* Hold your hand over the cards and tell the audience that you can sense each card's psychic vibrations.

Key card

Of course I'm psychic. I come from a family of psychotics.

*4* Square the deck, keeping the bottom card on the bottom.

*5* Fan the cards and have a volunteer choose one, hold it to his heart, and try to match his heartbeat to the psychic vibration of the card.

*6* Have the volunteer put his card on top of the deck, then cut the deck. Your key card is now on top of the chosen card.

*7* Ribbon spread the cards face up again.

*8* Have your volunteer point at the cards while you hold his wrist and move his finger along the ribbon. Tell the audience that you're searching for the card with vibrations that match the volunteer's pulse.

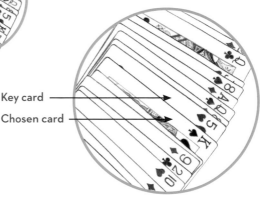

Key card ————

Chosen card ————

*9* Glance at the cards, looking for your key card. If you've spread the cards from left to right, the chosen card will be just to the right of the key card. If the key card is the last one in the ribbon, then the chosen card is the first one in the spread.

**You can cut the cards a hundred times in step 6 and this trick will still work.**

**Turn the page for the rest of the trick.**

*10* Don't stop when the volunteer's finger is pointing to his card. **Build the suspense.** Go to the end of the ribbon, then backtrack. Overshoot the card, and backtrack again. Finally, guide the volunteer's finger until it's touching the chosen card.

Sensing a card's (nonexistant) psychic vibrations isn't supposed to be easy. So make it look hard!

*11* Don't say anything for a moment. Then sweep away the cards on the right and on the left, leaving only the chosen card.

*12* Thank your volunteer for his deep understanding of vibrations. Take a bow as the crowd goes wild.

*You magically predict where a volunteer will cut the deck.*

# ALEX'S DOUBLE CROSS

**1** Fan the deck with the faces toward you. Notice the cards on the top and bottom of the deck. Pull out two cards that match these in rank and color. (If the end cards are a five of hearts and a queen of spades, pull out the five of diamonds and the queen of clubs.) Put the deck and the two cards face down on a table.

**2** Have a volunteer cut the deck and place the top half next to the bottom half.

Bottom half

Top half

**3** Take the bottom half and set it crosswise on the top half.

Say: "You cut the cards right here."

This trick works because of what magicians call a force. The volunteer thinks he can choose any cards, but you already know the cards he'll choose.

I predict a round of applause.

I predicted where you'd cut the cards.

**4** Point to the cards you chose earlier and say, "These cards will be the same color and rank as the cards you cut to."

**5** Pick up the top part of the deck. Take the bottom card and lay it face up on the table. Take the top card of the lower part of the deck and lay that face up.

**6** Turn over the cards you chose and — voilà! — a perfect match.

# WHAT'S NEXT?

**Every trick in this book gets better with practice. Can you do a one-hand cut without looking, spring the cards without thinking about it, toss a card up and catch it with ease? Keep practicing and you'll get there.**

You might try using flourishes in a casual, off-hand sort of way when you're playing cards. Do a riffle shuffle with a waterfall finish. Cut the cards with one hand.

Work on your patter (everything you say to the audience). Some say patter is the most important part of any trick. Practice your patter and know your lines before you perform.

Try your magic tricks on your family. (Be sure to practice first.) Think about where you can try a few magic tricks on your friends. Maybe in the cafeteria at lunchtime or when you're riding the bus.

I'd give my right arm to be ambidexterous.

One mind-reader said to the other, "You're fine, how am I?"

He who laughs last thinks slowest.

We've suggested a few ways to include flourishes and false shuffles in your magic tricks. Can you think of other ways to put some of these slick moves into your magic?

If there's a magic shop near where you live, you might want to stop by and say hello. Magic shops are great places to find other people who are interested in card stunts, card flourishes, and card magic. Practicing tricks in front of the mirror is good, but it's even better to practice with a friend, who can make suggestions about ways to improve your tricks.

And if you want to do more magic, we recommend **The Klutz Book of Magic** (which comes with five props so secret we can't even mention them here) and **Coin Magic** (which contains 24 coin tricks we should never have given away).

# Keep practicing. Have fun.

# Can't get enough?

Here are two simple ways to keep the Klutz coming.

**1** Get your hands on a copy of **The Klutz Catalog.**
To request a free copy of our mail order catalog, go to klutz.com/catalog.

**2** Become a **Klutz Insider** and get e-mail about new releases, special offers, contests, games, goofiness, and who-knows-what-all. If you're a grown-up who wants to receive e-mail from Klutz, head to klutz.com/insider.

If any of this sounds good to you, but you don't feel like going online right now, just give us a call at 1-800-737-4123. We'd love to hear from you.

## More Great Books from **KLUTZ**®

The Klutz Book of Magic

The Klutz Book of
Paper Airplanes

Explorabook®

Battery Science

The Solar Car Book

The Encyclopedia
of Immaturity

How to Make Monstrous,
Huge, Unbelievably
Big Bubbles

Quick Draw Flip Books

Coin Magic